GARDEN MAGIC

Phillip Watson

INTRODUCTION

When I was three years old and in a stroller, my mother and I happened to pass by a clump of blue German iris. She recently told me that I leaned forward to get a better view and said, "Pretty!" And, so it all began.

As I grew older, I learned to look for the spider lilies that seemed to pop up over night with no warning at all. I was always the first one in the family to find them and would run into the house to alert everyone.

My father once told me the story about my great aunt's favorite rose bush as I sat in awe. It had been brought to Mississippi on a wagon all the way from Virginia. I felt like I had been invited to join the cast of "Wagon Train", because I was *so* there…sitting at the front, holding that rose bush, and urging the horses onward.

For me the past is a companion who walks beside me as a gentle reminder of who I am, where I came from, and where I am going. Sometimes it winks at me like a lightening bug, and sometimes it sings to me like a wren.

Beyond our daily distractions is a world of beauty, full of nuance and enchantment. Mother Nature overlays everything with her ephemeral wrappings – a gift to us all. Colorful sunrises and sunsets, golden God Light, mysterious fog, and holiday frost add touches of glory in indiscriminate fashion.

The garden is full of such moments – some small as a hummingbird and some as extravagant as a flock of geese crossing in front of a full moon. On tranquil evenings, I still head out to my backyard, stretch out on the grass, and admire the thousands of stars spreading to infinity. I did this as a child, and it still beckons me. These private moments enhance my spiritual bonds and allow me to believe that everything will be alright.

GARDEN MAGIC, whose basic premise is to inspire rather than instruct, is my attempt to awaken the child in all of us – the one who delighted in finding the bird's nest in the hedge and enjoyed that single drop of nectar from a honeysuckle blossom. The reasons for wonderment haven't gone away, but our willingness to acknowledge them has faded. I hope this book will be a reminder that magic isn't a trick – it's real and just waiting to happen.

DEDICATION

GARDEN MAGIC is dedicated to my Facebook friends 📘
whose "likes" and comments led to the image choices…
and specifically to my mother and my sister,
without whom I would be less than whole.

www.facebook.com/phillipwatsondesigns

Magic isn't so much what you create, it's what you notice.

Phillip Watson

GARDEN MAGIC

THE GRAND SCHEME

Ah...the lap of luxury! Estate gardens are built upon the same principles as small gardens. They are simply larger and contain more features.

A variety of points of interest is as important to a garden as a variety of ingredients is to a good recipe. Why use iodized salt when you can use sea salt? Why use common phlox when you can use *Phlox paniculata* 'Peppermint Twist' (*right*).

Even grand gardens benefit from the kindness of strangers or being at the right place at the right time. In the distance is "the borrowed view" – glorious and oasis-like Long Island with The Sound in its foreground. A tall wall of clipped European hornbeam trees is perpendicular to the view, directing as opposed to blocking. In a smaller garden with less distinguished views, a simple six-foot fence will obscure your neighbors' weed lot while allowing you to enjoy the tops of their trees. As a good journalist might point out, the magic is in the editing.

These elaborate boxwood parterres (*right*) are connected and surrounded by flagstone pathways which evoke the feeling of a large plaza, ideal for entertaining. Patterns, in general, create interest whether they are boxwood patterns, paving patterns, or fence designs.

Bits of the garden which form the framework are often called "the bones". Without them the scene would be chaotic with little integrity during the growing season and none whatsoever during the winter months. I do believe that these parterres should be deemed "the elegant bones". And good bone structure is a hallmark of beauty.

Note the low pyramid at the left, covered in Boston ivy to give visual balance to the quadrants of the parterre garden. The building houses a home theatre and actually encroaches on one of the quadrants, but the blending of the green boxwoods with the green of the ivy cleverly disguises the discrepancy. Tricks of the trade.

The garden was designed for year-round interest, and its patterns, filled with annuals during the growing season, are often spangled with frost or dusted with snow during cold months. Purposely arranged as a low-slung and high-impact garden, these parterres do not detract from the view of Long Island Sound. On the other hand, I.M. Pei's Parisian Pyramid at the center of the Louvre's grand plaza does just the opposite: It obscures the long view and forces itself upon the viewer.

4

From the parterre gardens, a perfect lawn rolls out like a carpet as you make your way to the lily pond and the soothing sound of the cherub fountain. This large pool is filled with exotic aquatic plants as well as fancy goldfish (koi will eat your plants). Big planted pots are covered with gravel to secure the soil as well as the plants; cinder blocks, turned sideways, create tunnels and hiding places for the fish when herons and racoons approach. These raise the pots to the

> And here, on this delightful day,
> I cannot choose but think
> How oft, a vigorous man, I lay
> Beside this fountain's brink.
>
> *William Wordsworth*

desired level (six to eight inches below the surface of the water). Large ponds with plants and fish must be aerated and require filters as well as algae control.

The cast iron cherub was secured in Manhattan years ago and found its perfect home in this pond. As luck would have it, the fountain was cast the same year this home was built – 1939, the year of the Wizard of Oz.

Surrounding the fountain are the submerged container plantings of blue pickerel, variegated sedges, Egyptian papyrus, various water lilies, and pink flowering lotus.

The lotus flower symbolized the sun and the creation in Egyptian hieroglyphics. Egyptian culture also recognized the flower as a symbol of rebirth, and King Tut's tomb was prominently decorated with its image. Twelve-hundred year-old seeds have been sprouted, making them the oldest known viable seeds.

Many old estates have interesting outbuildings that were built in the same style as the main house. That fact alone makes it easier for the garden to appear to be an extension of the house. I am from Mississippi, and I adhere to the old Southern saying, "It's not done until it is overdone!" The lovely conical structure (*right*) has been outfitted with the equivalent of an ostrich feather boa – a festoon of fragrant white wisteria.

The same strategy may be used to tart up a utility shed or even a garage. Have you ever seen a top model without her makeup? Neither have I. Take a look at your outbuildings and see if they need an emergency make-over.

Pretty is as pretty does...

Whether your garden is on a grand scale or a small scale, it is your canvas. Some are as personal as a diary, and some are as blatant as a billboard. I try to strike a happy balance.

Several of these conical structures exist throughout this estate and are anchored by four-foot high stone walls which surround the main house, giving it a castle-like presence. Some are partially covered with climbing hydrangeas while others are clean. The architecturally clipped yews and boxwoods flank the egress points of the lily pond garden (*previous page*) – a nod to the stone pillars which guard the driveway entrances.

Wysteria, are your lips still lily-white?
Do they still bloom just at night and die at sunrise?
Dan Fogelberg

Whenever possible, look to the architecture for details to mimic or clip into shrubs and hedges. A solid and happy marriage of garden and house is the goal. Gimmicks seldom work beyond the honeymoon.

No, it's not a Christo art installation, but a clever way to wrap boxwoods for winter without losing the pattern. The same burlap covering is used on root balls. Here, strips are stitched together with long finishing nails as one might pin a hem. Who said burlap wasn't fashionable? Still…all dressed up and nowhere to go!

COTTAGE COMFORT

A cottage garden is, perhaps, the most intimate of all gardens and is often filled with heirloom plants (your grandmother's rose, the zinnias you grew from collected seeds, the daffodil bulbs you brought from your childhood home). As such, the garden tells a story that only you know. Sometimes it whispers to you, and sometimes it sings.

Unlike an estate garden, which is a collection of garden rooms (exterior spaces that are hedged or divided to create interesting compartments), a cottage garden is essentially one large garden room with a dwelling right in the middle of it. And rather than moving from room to room within the garden, you may move from room to room within the house while enjoying unique views from each window. This is not "the borrowed view", it is your private window to your little corner of the world.

Every garden may tell a story, but some gardens and gardeners have secrets.

When I was a child I looked forward to the daffodils and to that time of year in general. It meant dyed Easter chicks, soft clover for my bare feet, birds' nests full of colorful eggs, and bright blue skies.

As spring began to wane I looked all over the yard to see if I could find the last daffodil of the year. When I found it, I closed my eyes and inhaled the fragrance, memorizing the smell while thinking, "I won't see you again until next year."

> **I wandered lonely as a cloud**
> **That floats on high o'er vales and hills,**
> **When all at once I saw a crowd,**
> **A host of golden daffodils.**
>
> *William Wordsworth*

At sixteen my family and I moved from our small town to the seemingly large city of Jackson, Mississippi, and my life changed. Often, I returned to my hometown of Lexington to revisit the place that had made me, well, *me*. As I drove through the countryside I saw clumps and random beds of daffodils in the middle of the fields. Sometimes a chimney still stood, but those flowers were about the only reminders that a gardener had once lived there. I dug up several clumps and took them back to my new garden in Jackson where they made me a little less homesick.

Writers revisit old memories for inspiration and so do gardeners. Some memories are just too good to leave in the archives or in the middle of the fields.

Spring soon spills into summer, and other perennials emerge to take up the banner. Blue woodland phlox and peonies are perfect cover crops for seasoning daffodil foliage, as are daylilies. This is also the time to sow zinnia, cleome, and cosmos seeds. Without an augmentation of annuals, such as these, your garden display will be weak. Perennials alone will not carry the show.

Because a cottage garden is usually small, strategically placed flagstones are a good idea for easy access when weeding, watering, or gathering flowers for the house. The edges of the stones may be softened by planting the perennial golden creeping jenny or annuals such as alyssum and verbena.

Covering the walls of your cottage with vines (Boston ivy, in this case) is a good way to make the garden feel larger and, at the same time, more intimate. This is called vertical gardening, and it can be achieved with climbing hydrangea, English (evergreen) or Boston (deciduous) ivy, climbing roses, and clematis. The birds will move into those protected areas, and soon your garden really will sing to you.

Dwarf forms of old favorites are welcome additions to a cottage garden as long as their larger cousins are kept at bay. Lucky for us, the plant breeders have been quite busy, and there are now compact forms of helenium (*right*), salvia, foxgloves, hollyhocks, and even sunflowers.

Excluding all of your tall favorites isn't necessary, but proper management is. Staking is advised for summer phlox, true lilies, and other flowering plants that are inclined to sprawl…across the armrest and into your seat! Dead-heading will remove some of the weight from the ends of the stems to insure posture-perfect posies.

Another trick for creating height is to insert large pots directly into the garden beds. Cascading annuals such as petunias, sweet potato vines, and verbena hide the edges of the containers and contribute a seasonal dimension to this floral form of vertical gardening.

Other new notions on the horizon include "perpetuals", a top-tier class of perennials that bloom the entire season. Shasta daisies (White Mountain) that flower all summer? Why yes,

and also look for ever-blooming daylilies (Red Cardinal), coreopsis (Little Sundial), and agastache (Peachy Keen). Augment these storm troopers with your favorite annuals.

> **Were it not for confounding reality, my life would be a lark which I would pilot like a stunt plane.**
> *an excerpt from a sobering dream I had*

Read the plant labels and do your homework. What looks small the first year can triple in volume the second. Would you buy clothing without checking the size? It is fine to go to the nursery for ideas, but be careful what you select and *always* have a list. Remember the last time you went to the grocery store on an empty stomach? Even the cashier was appalled by the contents of your cart! Flights of fancy when coupled with reckless abandon can lead to garden disasters which often result in the loss of plants and sometimes entire growing seasons.

Keep in mind: Every open space is an opportunity for weeds. Plant accordingly, and enjoy the view.

A COUNTRY ESTATE

Country estates have the feel of that old leather chair you've had for years – a bit worn around the edges but sporting an authentic and rich patina that only time can bring. The lines of this garden are naturally blurred where they meet the woodland. The stone walls and edifices are embellished with lichen, and ancient warriors that were part of the original landscape plan now stand as gods in the garden.

This old Connecticut manor, known as Chelmsford, has such a pedigree. The main house was extended and refined by the venerable architectural firm of McKim, Mead, and White (Manhattan's original Pennsylvania Station, The Chicago World's Fair, Columbia University), and the gardens were lavishly designed by Charles Gillette, a Virginian, who was one of the top landscape architects of his day.

The house itself is perfectly situated atop a gentle knoll, and all of its rooms receive the kindest of ambient light.

At one time, Chelmsford was owned by Blanche Ferry, heir to the Ferry-Morse Seed Company. No doubt she and her family enjoyed the first fruits of new plant hybrids that put her father's seed company on the map. The original landscape plan shows an enormous vegetable garden, and the remnant of an old apple orchard still exists.

**Did you ever take a walk through the forest,
    stop and dream among the trees?
You can almost hear the voice of God
    in each and every breeze.**

Mac Davis

At its edges, the woodland had completely gone feral. Since one literally couldn't see the forest for the trees, much of the scruffy understory was removed and many of the trees were limbed up. This revealed an arboreal cathedral, setting the tone for what followed. A pervasive feeling of reverence is the common thread that runs throughout this gently rolling property.

Follies often exist on old properties, and this one has two. "The Aqueduct", as I call it, was built expressly as a folly and has no purpose other than to amuse and set the guests to wondering. This stone colonnade *(following page)* separates what was once the Ferry family's vegetable garden from the refined expanses of the cutting garden.

Its arches, which create windows into each room, offer "peak-a-boo, I-see-you" moments that add a fairy tale quality to the garden. The other folly, which is nearby, is the old root cellar where potatoes and turnips were once stored. These days, in its overgrown state, it looks more like the home of a hobbit. Children love this sort of thing as do adults who have never quite grown up.

It seems as though I am going from back to front, but in this "Alice In Wonderland" garden, it all makes sense. As one approaches the main house via a long circular drive, a heart-and-filigree parterre comes into focus. A recent embellishment, it adds a fresh touch to the old estate. In the foreground, a Japanese maple is in full color. He is one of the "gods of the garden" and shows up on the 1903 tree survey as "an old Japanese maple".

On the original landscape plans, the drive circle (now home to the parterre) was simply an oval green space. However, former owners had added a rock garden. I saw my chance to put my mark on the property, and I seized it. I also made sure my drawings were placed in the Chelmsford archives that contain Mr. Gillette's renderings.

Thankfully, I get to visit and stay at this old country estate regularly. Chelmsford still charms me, and it still has secrets, some of which I will never tell.

INTIMATE SPACES

Intimate spaces are those smaller areas of the garden which are somewhat private – like secret hideaways. Deep porches, like this one at Chelmsford, are a welcome sight and convey a feeling of hospitality.

Having a quiet refuge that isn't within the house provides a welcome break from the sounds of doors closing, children squabbling, and phones ringing. Sometimes you just need a moment to gather yourself. After your rejuvenation, you may just decide to stay on the porch.

Comfortable seating areas (don't forget the sofa) are ideal for relaxing alone with the newspaper or for entertaining a few friends. These areas conveniently offer an outdoor view of the garden that is under roof. I have taken many naps on this particular porch and have deemed it to be my favorite spot on Earth.

In my travels, I have seen countless exquisite gardens, but few are actually comfortable.

Most of my designing is done in the garden, not at the drafting table. I gather my dreams while enjoying the prevailing breezes, the smells of the garden, and the dancing light – even from a full moon. A client once asked, "Why do you sit in the garden in the pitch-black night?" Well, on a moonlit evening I simply see form and space. There are no colors or textures to seduce me and no shadows to fool me. At night I can see the garden for what it *needs* to be and where it should be structurally defined. First you build the house, and then you decorate it. So it is with the structure of the garden.

Since the dream for the garden was born beneath the stars, shouldn't there be an intimate spot for enjoying the completed fantasy?

When growing up in Mississippi, we had a home with second story sleeping porches, and I can still recall the excitement my siblings and I felt when an evening storm was brewing. As we listened to the distant thunder and the wind whipping through the old oak trees, we covered our heads with Daddy's old army blankets and shivered with glee!

From this particular porch in Connecticut, I have enjoyed the fragrance of climbing roses which frame its edges as well as a few glasses of champagne. Across the back garden I have watched the mountain laurels and peonies open in late May, and I have seen the sparrows make

Today while the blossoms still cling to the vine,
I'll taste your strawberries,
    I'll drink your sweet wine.
                                    New Christy Minstrels

nests behind the gutters. By October, the maples in the distance have begun to catch fire with their fall colors, and soon the house will be decorated for its annual Christmas party. On the less frigid days of winter the porch still beckons, and this time of year blankets are provided – just not army blankets.

Some places and some flowers remind you of long ago happy moments the same way that old friends remind you of who you are in case you forget.

Chelmsford certainly doesn't suffer from shyness. This circus tent-like pool house is all ready for the guests to arrive. It is, in fact, original to the house as is the pool. Both were simply refurbished and given a dandy new look. A gurgling fountain was added at the pavilion end of the pool to add a bit of water music. The entire structure is hidden from the previously mentioned porch view by a large ellipse of hemlock trees, and as one enters the pavilion, it is quite a happy surprise.

Like the porch, it is suitable for entertaining even in winter. It has a huge fireplace…and a sound system…and a bar…and the pool is heated!

The beds that surround the pool peninsula are filled with fragrant spring-blooming French lilacs and rose-scented peonies. With plenty of lounge chairs nearby, this perfumed oasis delivers comfort and privacy as well as the opportunity for a midnight dip.

Pool peninsulas (*pictured*), terraces, and elevated decks offer ideal perspectives for viewing the garden. A change of grade in the garden is as effective as a change of key in a song. Parterres especially look more impressive when viewed from above. Who wouldn't want the catbird seat? Another bonus: At higher levels, breezes are more likely, and bugs are less likely.

These intimate garden spaces are just a few steps further into the garden than the porches and pavilions mentioned earlier in this chapter. Although these garden rooms have no roofs, they are close enough to structures for weather-related mad dashes.

Of course, it's better to be prepared. Garden umbrellas come in a variety of colors and patterns which give a "we're on vacation" look to the garden. Just remember to lower them on windy days to avoid a Mary Poppins moment.

My eyes can dimly see
The pattern of my life
And the puzzle that is me.

Paul Simon

Patterns, in general, put everything into sharp focus whether the subject is candy cane striped draperies, the back of a Chinese chippendale chair, or a boxwood parterre. Don't be dull; the butter knife already has that job.

Decorating and furnishing the garden room, whether it is a deck, a terrace, or a walled space, should be fun. Use the same exuberance you mustered when developing your flower borders, and the only thing left will be to send the invitations. Bright colors, bold patterns, music, lights, action!

Garden vestibules and floral corridors are living extensions of the home and serve the same purposes as their like-named cousins within. The most successful designs mirror the architectural flavor and palette of the home. This boxwood framed "vestibule" takes dramatic advantage of light quality as the evergreen shrubs are diamond-cut to create facets. If they were simply round as most boxwoods, they wouldn't sparkle. Let me see…a lump of coal or a diamond? Gosh, it's just so hard to choose!

Within this small entry garden is a spacious brick patio which leads to the front door landing. Notice how the flat-topped boxwoods and their sloping sides nicely mimic the lines of the home's roof. A long antique bench provides an elegant focal point as well as a spot for husbands to wait for wives who can't tear themselves away from the party.

A pair of cast iron urns, which are the same flat black as the shutters, flank the front door and are easily filled with seasonal plants.

Reflecting the white of the main house, an avenue of 'Annabelle' hydrangeas connects this entry garden to a treillage-enclosed garden via a generously scaled brick pathway that is gently lit for evening strolls. Inside the intimate space of this elegant garden room are herbs for the kitchen and cut flowers for the rest of the house. Note the fence details which subtly echo the railings on the top of the house.

The interior space of the treillage garden is basically a large parterre consisting of boxwood-lined beds and brick pathways. Even in winter, the beds are well-defined and provide a pleasing view from the master bedroom on the second floor of the home.

Spring finds this intimate enclosure ablaze with daffodils and tulips. As the 'Annabelle' hydrangeas begin their show in June, the yellow heliopsis daisies *(following pages)* follow suit. Right on their heels are hardy red salvias, blue balloon flowers, and summer phlox. Were it not for the strict geometry of the plan, the space would look like a cottage garden. However, it has been disciplined.

A perfect example of green architecture, this garden is on the same grid as the house, has many of the same elements as an architectural plan, and flows as seamlessly as a cocktail party.

Classic and Southern, this walled garden's gates are lit by gas lanterns. It isn't just a horticultural extension of the house, it is actually part of the architecture. Seven-foot stucco walls, which match the house, surround its front and sides with strategically placed openings for comfortable access to and from the garden rooms waiting within. To the right of the main entrance a large urn filled with variegated ginger welcomes guests and serves as a counter balance to the tower at the left.

The pierced gate permits a preview of the garden even before it is opened. A *little* teasing is acceptible in Southern culture. The flagstone path begins as a walkway that is parallel to the front walls of the house, leads to the front gate, and flows into a large courtyard. From the front gate, the gurgling of the large fountain seductively beckons. Of course, climbing plants have to be included! In this case, native and evergreen cross vine (Bignonia) embraces the columns and adds a bit of woolliness for a softer and less austere approach.

Once inside *(following pages)*, palms and palmetto dance in the breeze around the central fountain whose partial shade is afforded by a live oak adjacent to the main tower. At its base are white caladiums which brighten the area even at night. The evergreen conifers lining the wall to the right are clipped in such a way as to allow shafts of light to flow from one room to the next and to reveal similar glimpses as the pierced main gate.

Remember…life is just a memory.
Remember…close your eyes and you can see.
Harry Nilsson

The central fountain is the largest within the walled garden, but there are several others which produce audible guidance from room to room. All of these fountains are lit beneath the water surface which overlays all in a romantic glow.

62

The side entrance to this enchanting garden is just as beautiful as the main entrance and leads departing guests to a private parking area. Gas lanterns light the way into the night, which always ends on a high note – even when no wine is served.

The footprint of these walled gardens is equivalent to the interior space of the entire first floor of the home. Large windows, which scarcely need curtains, provide spectacular and private views of the garden rooms that wrap the dwelling.

Can you imagine having an entirely private and secure garden? On mild days, the doors and windows can be left open, and even parties may spill out into the garden. There is a distinct New Orleans vibe that is further punctuated by the white stucco surfaces which have taken on a French Quarter patina. Oh, for a beignet!

Garden "walls" can be made of many things at whatever level is desired. Clipped boxwoods and low brick knee walls serve the same purpose in defining a space and still promote views beyond.

If these views beyond are unsightly, tall hedges of arborvitae or privacy fences may be desired. Windows can be cut into either of these for specific vantage points or as teases for the next garden room.

Unlike large garden areas, small intimate spaces have no room for mistakes. Plants or hardscape items that only look good from a distance have no place here, and beautiful, thoughtful design is critical.

Close quarters mean close scrutiny, and all of the seats in this small horticultural theatre are front row. Interesting plant choices help to raise the bar, followed by the clever design elements of pathways, furniture, containers, and other focal points. Splurge on a fabulous garden bench the same way you might justify buying an expensive mirror for a powder room. The space is small and doesn't require much in terms of volume, but it does require a lot in terms of style.

A FANTASY GARDEN

"The plane! The plane!"

No, it isn't Fantasy Island, but it did take a plane to capture this Whitman Sampler-type opening image.

As mentioned earlier, perspective is key when viewing certain types of gardens, and patterned gardens such as this one are simply breathtaking when admired from above. Of course, the views from the bedroom windows aren't too shabby either.

As one enters the property, an avenue of clipped linden trees, up-lit for dramatic effect, sets the stage for what promises to be quite a show. Immediately ahead is a perfectly balanced architectural marvel which sparkles like a mirage. There are many things on this Earth that look too good to be true, but this is as real as it gets and as good as it gets for a garden designer who would like to make a statement.

Sometimes things are not what they appear to be within a garden, and many rely upon tricks and gimmicks for attention. It is hard to take a garden seriously if it is simply a string of punchlines.

Enchantment comes from within and is child-like in its purity. Seduction, while tantalizing, comes from an external source and can be rife with deception.

The truth of the matter is, this garden does indeed have it all – a grand swimming pool in perfect proportion to the house, long expansive flower borders filled with unusual treasures, a wetland habitat of bald cypress, deciduous holly, swamp mallow and Louisiana iris, elaborate formal parterres, a garden-enclosed tennis court, a walled potager full of heirloom vegetables, and a guest cottage that presents itself as an oasis. Some gardens have bells and whistles; this garden has a full orchestra.

Now, travel with me from the stark and dramatic contrasts of the front garden to the uninhibited exuberance of the side and rear gardens. We shall touch all of the bases and slide into home!

Like the equal and paired front parterres, the side gardens are mirror images of one another and provide that change of key which makes this tune particularly interesting. Matching porches flank both ends of the house and are accessed by a series of bluestone steps and landings. Bordering the stairs from top to bottom are abundantly planted peony beds. The varieties consist of early, mid, and late spring bloomers, many of which are rose-scented ('Gold Standard', 'Mons. Jules Elie', 'Gay Paree'). Staggered varieties results in a full month of peony blooms. Notice how the peony blooms drape over the edges of the steps, creating a "Stairway to Heaven" feel. Also, unsightly stakes and ties aren't necessary with this cozy relationship of peony and pavement. Keep this in mind: single and semi-double peonies stand up better than the big pom-pom varieties.

Prior to the arrival of the peonies, daffodils bloom within the same footprint and herald the arrival of a new season. After those early bloomers finish, their seasoning yellow foliage is quickly engulfed by the emerging peonies. Another plus: deer will not eat daffodils or peonies.

After the peony blooms have faded and have been removed, the dark green foliage remains as a dense, leafy border well into autumn. Fertilize it immediately after bloom time to keep it lustrous. Tall salvias (also deer-proof) may be added within the beds for summer and fall blooms if desired.

I try to live in moderation,
but that only gives me aggravation.
Shemekia Copeland

But speaking of foliage, notice the loose dark-leafed tree that slightly overhangs this garden. It is a 'Bloodgood' Japanese maple whose burgundy foliage adds great interest to the surrounding green canopies and is a lovely complement to the brightly hued peonies. In the far distance is an echo of that same dark foliage – a purple beech that is over one hundred years old. The pieces of the puzzle are coming together; some bits are bold and some, like these, are subtle.

Following the month-long performance of the rose-scented peonies, the *real* roses kick in. Shall we make our way across the upper landing to see what lies beyond?

Huge beds of red and pink 'Knockout' roses *(previous page)* stretch the entire length of the back of the home, and their dazzling display of eye-popping color is visible from all of the rear windows. These particular roses bloom well past Halloween and are the lowest maintenance of any roses available. With rose gardens it is important to adjust the varieties to match your maintenance skills. A low boxwood edging just above the stone knee wall defines and contains the beds much like a thick rope of icing at the base of a cake.

At the center of the upper landing, a four-tiered wire plant stand holds court with an assortment of bromeliads whose six-inch pots have been hidden by Spanish moss. These are easily changed out to suit the season or the party. For Easter it held pots of tulips and daffodils with a moss-covered bunny at the top. I resisted the temptation to hide eggs in it...

Front and center is a perfectly square swimming pool (44' x 44') whose dark bottom enables it to settle into the landscape with ease – enhancing, not overpowering. Adjacent flower beds hold a panoply of perennials including several types of agastache, asclepias, and trumpet lilies, all of which are magnets for butterflies.

Uniting the rear garden is a huge limestone terrace which connects the house, surrounds the pool, and leads to the treillage-winged pavillion. The "wings" are actually arbors which are covered with blue, pink, and white wisteria vines. In late spring they erupt in a profusion of perfumed blossoms, and their leafy canopy provides shade throughout the summer when pool parties are in full swing.

Beneath the arbors and beyond are color-coordinated seating areas which deliver comfort as well as style. The green of the umbrellas matches the green of the Moroccan tile walls inside the pool house, and that is precisely where I am heading.

Within this fanciful, vaguely Cape Dutch structure are changing rooms as well as a fully stocked kitchen. Natural light bathes the interior via an open central passageway, and guests may gather here for cocktails or an informal buffet along the spacious stainless steel bar.

Just steps away from the pavillion is a picket-enclosed vegetable garden *(following pages)*. This nicely appointed potager provides produce for the table throughout the summer, and its fences keep out hungry rabbits. Heirloom tomatoes, colorful peppers, salad greens of all sorts, and various herbs abound. Fresh mint for iced tea is kept under control by keeping it in a pot.

I wish my maternal grandfather were still alive so we could talk vegetables. When I was a child, I played in his warehouse which was full of big croaker sacks of vegetable seeds. Granddaddy owned Service Seed Company in Crystal Springs, Mississippi, and brokered and shipped huge orders of fresh tomatoes, peppers, and other vegetables. The sorting and packing sheds were right by the train tracks. However, by the mid 1950s, plant viruses ended Crystal Springs' run as "The Tomato Capitol of the World" and the geneticists had to begin working on solutions.

Today we are blessed with heirloom tomatoes on grafted and disease-resistant root stock. Two large pots on a patio will give you more tomatoes than you can eat, and those pithy grocery store varieties can stay right where they are. Diets aren't nearly so arduous when the food tastes good!

An edible garden can be many things. I often sow lettuce seeds in my flower borders to fill in the gaps. It's beautiful, adds texture, and gives a whole new meaning to "the edible landscape." In late summer those same flower borders receive an infusion of rainbow chard and frilly kale. It looks good enough to eat, and that is exactly what I do.

Keep it simple and only grow the things you eat often. Also, check with your neighbors before planting. Only one person per street needs to grow zucchini! As for tomatoes, try the heirlooms for flavor, and for high yield take a look at the new grafted tomato plants. It's all about the flavor. Some days lunch is fancy; on other days that perfect tomato sandwich awaits. Mmmm!

BOUNTIFUL BORDERS

Flower borders are basically the tail of the peacock. The rest of the bird is mighty pretty but, goodness gracious, would you look at that! If parterres and other clipped plants are the bones of the garden, the flowers are certainly the muscles. And "flower power" packs quite a punch.

When putting together a border simply follow good planting guidelines and remember, you are the boss. Do you think that great artists consult the color wheel before dipping their brushes into the paint? Matisse was famous for using clashing colors in perfect harmony. It's all about volume and proportion. The garden canvas is no different. The flower border may be just the spot to show others that you really aren't dull...

Be bold and confident in your plant selections, but even if you have a pretty good grasp of horticulture, always read the plant tags. You may know salvias, for instance, but they may range in height from ten inches to over five feet. Before you can sing, you must first learn the scales.

When I initially visited the estate, the large lawn area sloped down to the woods. A four-foot retaining wall was added at the edge of the property and backfilled to create the smooth surface of turf. This bit of engineering resulted in an "infinity pool" look for the flower border perched above it. Superb drainage and good air circulation seal the deal for this picture perfect situation.

Frequent breezes make the border literally dance, and certain plants were chosen for their prowess. Blue salvias, which appear to be reaching for the sky, are sturdy as well as flexible and know how to "get down"! They also know how to get back up and seldom require staking. Should some of the dancers get out of hand, a rolling fog is often at hand to provide a bit of modesty.

Densely planted borders rarely require much in the way of staking as neighbors tend to hold one another up, much like the "painted ladies" row houses in San Francisco. 'Fireworks' goldenrod is a perfect companion for the blue salvias as well as the 'Grape Nectar' agastache, 'Golden Delicious' pineapple sage, and 'Señorita Rosalita' cleome, all of which are deer-proof.

Bold choices yield exciting and unexpected results. If you are simply afraid to have a good time, then we may have a problem…

A small tidy garden is certainly preferable to a large messy one. If you have a mansion and can't afford a maid, you should start looking for a condo! Remember, perfect gardens come in all sizes, so make sure your dream garden fits your personal reality. Life itself is like a garden, and some lives have more weeds than flowers. However, if you plant enough flowers, there is little room for weeds.

Gardening is that magical convergence of art, science, and gambling. Huge dividends are rarely paid out on risk-free investments. Be smart *and* daring. Study the plant catalogues, visit good public gardens and arboretums, read those plant tags, and set up a maintenance schedule that fits your sensible plan. By all means, tour your garden on a daily basis. If that seems unappealing, it is because your garden isn't provocative enough. Turn up the fire!

While touring your flower border, don't forget to dead-head, which promotes more blooms. Also, if old blossoms (particularly roses) are allowed to simply drop to the ground, disease problems can develop. Notice if certain plants might appreciate staking or if weeds are threatening to overtake one of your favorites. Mulching is a good way to cut down on an overabundance of weeds, and a pre-emergent will keep their seeds from germinating. If you are sowing flower seeds in the border, avoid the pre-emergent.

None of these tasks, which will save time and plants in the long run, are overly difficult. My dad once told me that when he got depressed, he simple dug a ditch until it passed. *We*, however, will dig flower beds because being busy keeps crazy in the corral...

When I design my clients' borders, I always consider the maintenance. If a staff of gardeners is available, I let loose and give them plenty to maintain. However, if my client isn't so inclined, I put forth a plan that will bring beauty and pleasure, not anxiety and disaster. Know your limits and either expand them or garden within them. There's that confounding reality, again!

Huge sweeps of even the commonest flowers are simply glorious to see. This effect can be achieved with bulbs, perennials, and annuals. I use all of these in grand gestures.

For the budget conscious, entire beds can be filled from seed with annuals such as cosmos, cleome, four o'clocks, and zinnias. These selections are deer resistant and will bloom their heads off all summer and well into fall. Simply scatter them across the tops of your clean new beds or even among perennials in old ones.

I build my new beds in the fall so the bulbs can go right in, and the seeds can be sown after they finish blooming in spring. Don't wait until spring to make the beds, because you just might not get around to it. My personal thought is this: Procrastination is Purgatory – like putting your happiness on layaway and never making the final payment. And, a defaulted garden is simply a weed lot.

Daffodil bulbs are by far the best investment as they multiply and are immune to pests. Having a colorful and fragrant fanfare to end winter is the reward we all need. Your perennials or seeded annuals will cover the aging daffodil foliage, so there will be none of that nonsense like braiding the leaves. Who thinks of these things?

116

GOD LIGHT

The most ephemeral magic is the all-embracing mantle of gold known as God Light. Suddenly it appears, and just as suddenly it is gone. Occurring on rare occasions, this golden light can precede or follow storms – especially just before dusk when the sun is finally low enough to find that narrow window between the horizon and the base of the cloud cover. As it streaks across the bottoms of the clouds, it bounces light off their uneven surfaces and gilds everything in its path from west to east. Sometimes this special light finds small holes in the cloud cover and sneaks in as single beams. Old religious paintings often show angels floating down on those heavenly rays, hence the term "God Light".

A shimmering weeping willow, which was planted many years ago to commemorate the birth of a child, is particularly stunning in its King Midas spotlight. When something is this beautiful, the moment doesn't have to last long for it to be memorable. This "Tree of Life" was moved from

the first house to its current location when the child was six. Now, the child is nearly a man.

Quiet beauty such as the reflection in a small puddle, an overhead flock of sunlit geese, or the sound of the wind in the willow is meant for those who are grateful for the natural wonders that surround us each day. They comfort and enchant. This isn't a land of make believe, it is a superb level of awareness where "alone" doesn't mean "lonely".

**Life, so they say, is but a game
and they let it slip away.
Love, like the autumn sun, should be
dying, but it's only just begun.**
Seals and Crofts

Light quality can drive painters to paint and dreamers to dream, and for centuries artists and writers have been drawn to certain areas of the world for that reason. What would Vermeer's paintings have been like without his masterful representations of light?

Perfect illumination turns simple things into treasure and levels the playing field for even the weeds. However, sometimes a star is singled out *(previous page)* for a three minute solo, such as this glowing weeping willow.

124

Even before summer slides into fall, the landscape can glow as if autumn hues had prematurely arrived. The following trick is for those who are too distracted to notice fleeting ephemerals.

This border (*right*) is ablaze thanks to the use of highly contrasting foliage. All good gardens have gorgeous flowers, but only great gardens have gorgeous foliage. Glowing orbs of the pineapple sage, 'Golden Delicious', punctuate the flower border from end to end, resulting in a God-like version of heavenly light that is only possible because of plant selection. The leaves smell just like fresh pineapples, and in October bright red flower spikes crown the plants. Lingering hummingbirds appreciate this last supper before heading south for winter.

The dark red foliage at the far end of the border is a group of 'Crimson Pigmy' barberry shrubs which act as artificial shadow. The border design dazzles the eyes even on cloudy days. The shadow and light duel of the golden sage and the crimson barberry creates a cadence that is a visual mirage. Imagine for a moment that all of the foliage in the border is green. I do believe the music just stopped…

Is that a red flag waving in the distance? Apparently the party isn't over…it continues within the stately white barn (*previous page*) which was repurposed for after-hours revelry. The structure, built in England in 1810, was shipped to this property in the early part of the twentieth century. The red "flag" at its eastern end is a decades-old Japanese maple in full flame. Beneath the billowing crimson leaves, an antique iron bench awaits.

As "God's gilding" streams from the west, long shadows creep across the land, filling its nooks and crannies like so many ink wells. Above these darkened depths, the surfaces sparkle as if the vaults of Ft. Knox had been thrown open.

Patterns, like this boxwood parterre, come alive and constitute a stylish foil for "the borrowed view" of conservancy land that lies beyond. Notice the single white dash of oyster shell path at the center. After the light show is over, that white path, which weaves throughout the gardens, will still be shining.

The trees of the forested horizon are all aglow as day bids adieu, and even the bare sycamore limbs gleam like alabaster. I tend to remember quiet moments like this more vividly than anything else. Sitting still doesn't necessarily mean that nothing is happening.

> There's a star on the far horizon, rising
> bright in an azure sky.
> For the rest of the time that you're given,
> why walk when you can fly.
>
> *Mary Chapin Carpenter*

When I was in college working towards a degree in horticulture, I took up water coloring as a way to remember the different types of trees. My first subjects were individual leaves – all in fall glory. As I studied each leaf I examined the veins, every blotch and blemish, and even the ways the stems attached themselves. I never looked at the forest in the same way again.

133

As the pierced chimneys of this home pinpoint sequestered views of the moon, the eastern porch provides a panoramic painting of the season – not just scores of trees, but millions of sparkling leaves that change with the light, the wind, and the season. I would rather miss an episode of a favorite show than a day of this. These fleet-footed moments are not available as re-runs.

Do you have a gorgeous picture of yourself that was taken outside? Usually it is the light quality that enhances the moment. Even though "God Light" is seemingly bright, it has a softness that produces a glow, minimizes flaws, and puts shadows in just the right places.

Dusk brings with it that time known as "The Magic Hour". Nature artist, Walter Anderson, was fond of painting at that time. He had a small artist's shack on Horn Island just off the Mississippi Gulf Coast. As mentioned earlier, artists *and* photographers gravitate towards ambient light. Garden photographers know when to visit gardens and can be seen before dawn and right at dusk. They are not working *their* magic, they are attempting to capture what nature has so perfectly lit.

> I am walking through the silver morning, and I feel the music inside me.
>
> *Kenny Rankin*

Morning light, just before sunrise, is equally flattering but instead of gold, has a silver quality. Sometimes it is accompanied by morning fog which bounces the rays around like phosphorescence.

Like the millions of gilded leaves in the distance, the flowers of the borders shine. Look closely and examine the petals. Having an artist's eye doesn't make you an artist, but it does help you to appreciate art. God is in the details.

ON A SALT MARSH

Perfection comes in all sizes and, in some cases, knows no boundaries. Again, we visit "the borrowed view" which stretches to the horizon, crosses a salt marsh delta, and includes a distant hardwood forest. This cove-facing garden is the playground for all sorts of wildlife including red-winged blackbirds, migratory seabirds, and resident raptors like the magnificent osprey.

My clients said to me, "You will be disappointed when you see our small property. It is nothing like the estates you are used to." Well, "disappointed" didn't even cover it...I was simply enchanted! Mother Earth served as my mentor as I set about designing the garden. The physical property is not large, but the views beyond are breathtaking, and I just needed to reel them in.

Lining this salt water cove are marsh grasses which move like parting hair as the tides go in and out. Above all of this float the seabirds, either in formation or diving for today's fresh catch.

This charming aerie, just off Long Island Sound, sits high above the marsh and is protected by old stone walls that keep tidal surges from overtaking the property. The garage, which is built in the same coastal style as the house, has a waterside port beneath it. Kayaking is the game, and birdwatching is the aim. The husband, who is a superb photographer and quick on the draw, captured a rainbow as well as a busy osprey. Such ephemerals are often missed, they happen so quickly.

Red and yellow and pink and green,
Purple and orange and blue.
I can sing a rainbow, I can sing a rainbow,
I can sing a rainbow, too.

The Dells

Being aware of your surroundings isn't just for safety, it can nourish the soul. Once you are able to tune in to the songs of the birds and gaze in awe at a multi-colored sunrise, you are well on your way to a better life.

At the overlook, I designed a stone perch for elbows, cameras, and wine glasses. This vantage point has a ledge under it for an oblong planter of "hens and chicks" which turn a deep burgundy just in time for the holidays.

Below the parapet wall is an old sculptural red oak whose branches fan out loosely over the marsh as well as the terrace. That one tree effectively bridges the gap between civilization and raw nature. From its broad branches hang an assortment of bird feeders that are not lacking for customers and above on a higher limb is the osprey's dining room. Yes, trout was on the menu, today!

The terrace, which consists of two levels, is, figuratively speaking, a theatre. The upper level patrons may enjoy lunch or cocktails while watching the ever-changing show that is the salt marsh. The lower level garden is open for business during intermission.

The surfaces of this first level garden are fitted with large flat field stones whose hard edges disappear in a carpet of Dichondra 'Silver Falls', golden creeping jenny, purple verbena, and white alyssum. This "tapestry walk" takes foot traffic in stride and is a magnet for butterflies who use its stone steps as basking rocks. Adjacent to this tapestry are beds holding the ever-durable magenta astilbe (feather flower), variegated Japanese iris, climbing pink roses, and that ol' warhorse, Agastache 'Blue Fortune'.

Nearby are the deep pink rugosa roses whose hips (the seeds) are known as "sea tomatoes". They are higher in vitamin C than oranges. These thorny clove-scented roses spread by suckers, and colonies of them are commonly found on coastal sand dunes where they help control erosion. Prickly roses discourage those who might be tempted to get too close to the edge of the wall. Ouch!

Assorted ornamental grasses line the tops of the sea wall and sway in the breeze with the cattails below. Their already golden plumes catch the last rays of the autumn day and become one with the river of aquatic grasses that spreads to The Sound.

In this coastal habitat, one may enjoy the changing of the seasons in a multitude of ways, and even the daily tidal flows bring unexpected reasons to be happy.

The migratory osprey – what a creature to see! With camera in hand, the owner of this habitat garden is always ready to record those moments of migrating and resident sea birds. The occasional rainbow is the icing on the cake, and being on a salt marsh is akin to being part of a magic show – Abracadabra!

INTO THE WOODS

Some gardens are designed as habitats, but a woodland *begins* as a habitat. The goal should be to enhance rather than to compromise its relationship with nature. A certain unruliness prevails, but this unbridled behavior can be liberating, especially for those who are weary of such traditional tasks as weeding, pruning, fertilizing, and spraying. Mother Nature is a pretty smart gal, and she will work her magic if her hands aren't tied.

Resist the compulsion to remove the fallen leaves in autumn or to cut down every dead tree. Those leaves, which act as a natural mulch, provide a cushion against heavy rains and reduce erosion.

Of course the smell of autumn leaves adds an olfactory element that can stir childhood memories of playing in piles of them. Remember those sweet clouds of smoke that arose when the leaf piles were burned?

Dead or dying trees are fine as long as they don't spread insect problems or diseases and are in no danger of falling on visitors. Remove over-hanging hazardous limbs and leave the trunk as a natural feeder and nest site for woodpeckers and other drilling birds. These transitional bits of the woodland provide opportunities for wildlife and opportunities for visitors with cameras.

Treat the woodland like a giant garden home that has high ceilings, wide hallways, windows with views, and lots of good art. The tree canopy can easily be raised to give ample head room for visitors and to allow for better lighting for the understory plants. "Furniture" can consist of

> When you're feeling down and out,
> Wondering what this world's about
> I know a place that has the answer.
> *Chuck Mangione,* Land of Make Believe

swings between trees, rustic benches, or even large logs. Those "hallways" and paths should be slightly elevated to maintain a dry corridor. For this eight-foot-wide path, a bed of crushed gravel was put down first (a crown of 10" at the center) and a 5" layer of shredded cypress mulch was spread across the top. The cypress mulch is very slow to decompose, resulting in a soft and quiet corridor. A noisy path scares off the wildlife waiting for you and your camera. No need to walk softly *and* carry a big stick…this is the tame woodland!

157

Certain areas of the woodland can be rough or even boggy. Low boardwalks may be used to traverse these areas. Don't miss the chance to employ wetland plants such as Louisiana iris, sedges, deciduous swamp holly or, in this case, big stands of palmetto palms (for Southern regions, only). These are the same sorts of boardwalks found in nature preserves, and their weathered surfaces blend nicely with the bark of the surrounding trees. Gaining access to natural habitats is a tricky business, and a minimalist approach is generally favored. This is one of the few cases where less is actually more.

The bridge and fountain (*featured on the next two pages*) were fashioned from building rubble. Their palomino-like patterns mirror the dappled light of the forest floor. Notice how the bridge bed is covered in the same mulch as the path. Manmade structures can look foreign in a naturally styled garden setting, but these additions don't subtract from the beauty of a perfect marriage of forest and folly.

The gurgling stream is really a large recirculating fountain whose pump and liner have been concealed by carefully laid river rocks and strategically located plants. Some of the waterside plants are native species, but many are fancy versions of them. I am not a huge fan of tricks in the garden, but this "natural" stream gets my vote.

Beyond this folly is the romantically illuminated forest understory. Once trees have been limbed up and skylights have been incised, enough light should stream down to encourage shade-loving shrubs and perennials.

The cultivated woodland is a super concentrated version of nature and requires thoughtful design and specific maintenance. While weeding and pruning are somewhat minimum, keeping certain plants under control is still important. Keep an eye out for over-performing "thugs" which can engulf colonies of smaller and slower growing plants. If the aggressive plants are allowed to take over, the garden will be less interesting. For a garden to have a big personality, it must also have many facets. In this case, more IS more and less is, well, skimpy.

Whether the woodland garden has a man-made fountain or a natural body of water, the results are charming. The wild creatures of the garden appreciate these features as much as the human visitors and depend on them as part of their viable habitat. Set up your bird feeders and benches nearby so the winged ones aren't the only ones with a bird's-eye view.

Koi fish are commonly associated with Chinese culture as well as the artful science of feng shui. These colorful fish represent good fortune, longevity, ambition, and perseverance – qualities which are necessary to be a successful life-long gardener.

A PRIVATE RETREAT

My private retreat isn't really a retreat at all. It gives me strength and inspiration which allow me to move forward. Here, there is an amplification and refinement of all things personal and precious. Each plant has a story, and that is the sweet mystery of this refuge.

The four o'clocks that I planted from seed are a reminder of my childhood when my best friend, Sammy, and I played Tarzan in a field that was full of them. Their fragrance still transports me. My grandfather is out there, too, in the form of a pheasant's eye daffodil that he loved so much. And over there is Aunt Julia, all dressed up like a rose! This garden, which is my secret friend, keeps me company and keeps me grounded. I know its parts, its seasons, its moods, and its quirks. My garden and I are in a long-term committed relationship.

I must have arrived in Pennsylvania in a daze, because I didn't even know I had bought the same house twice. One evening I was heading for the basement stairs when I had a déja vu moment. I suddenly realized that the entire floor plan was exactly the same as my first home in Fredericksburg, Virginia, right down to the window placements and dormers.

We are certainly creatures of habit and gravitate towards the familiar. Next to the garage of this old stucco house is a deep pink camellia shrub whose presence surprised me when I first visited the property. I grew up with them in Mississippi and saw that as a good omen. I bought the house that same day.

"Something old, something new…" Well, my something new was a variegated weeping dogwood (*Cornus kousa* 'Kristin Lipka') which I embellished with a climbing pink clematis vine. Nearby are two stone benches from my first home in Virginia. A lush stand of ostrich ferns completes the tableaux.

In early spring the camellia is in full bloom, and I flash back to the times I spent at my grandmother's house. She named seedling camellias (many simply came up beneath the mother plant) after all of her grandchildren. As the blooms loosen and drop to the ground, a rich carpet of crimson forms. And as she did, I gather some to float in a bowl on my dining table.

Sometimes I fill a box top with camellia blooms to share with a neighbor who invariably brings me a cake or a pie the next day!

The feathery wisps of pink and white astilbe (*following pages*) adorn the garden shortly after the camellias exit the stage and supply the first perennial blossoms of the season. Their leaves closely resemble those of the adjacent ferns and add a softness that one expects from springtime. As if on cue, the robins arrive and quickly set about gathering thatch and mud to construct their sturdy nests which will soon hold those "robin's egg blue" treasures.

I'm thrilled to see the wrens moving into the birdhouses scattered about the property and have heard the peeper frogs warming up their voices at dusk. Take time to notice. There's a lot going on that will charm you. Have you ever seen a hummingbird moth? Well, plant some Verbena bonariensis and you will.

A friend once remarked, "I am so sad because my hummingbirds have left for the season." To have enjoyed, to have noticed are reasons to be happy, not sad. They will be back next year to enjoy their favorites: salvias, verbenas, morning glories, and lantana. In the meanwhile, luxuriate in the afterglow. It is yours to embrace.

> Will somebody wear me to the fair?
> Will a lady pin me in her hair?
> Will a child find me by a stream?
> Kiss my petals and weave me through a dream.
>
> Les Fleurs *as sung by Minnie Riperton*

My private retreat is so private that I don't even have curtains. Initially, work on the garden entailed screening it from the road and the neighbors. Once that was achieved, I set about creating pockets of interest that I could appreciate from the windows of my home. Strategically placed birdhouses, fragrant dwarf lilacs beneath the bathroom window, fiery red Sunpatiens that match the front door, early blooming daffodils within the walled garden…there's so much to enjoy, and I do.

Those magic creatures who make their homes within the garden or who are occasional visitors, add an ephemeral layer that outshines all of the flowers. Your children will notice them before you do. Somehow we get so distracted as we age that we miss all of the things that used to make our hearts sing. Daredevil butterflies and courting birds are putting on a show for most of the season, and you have season tickets. Use them!

Life is full of ephemerals as is the garden. The German iris bloomed for a scant few days, but the memory of their unfurling beauty stays until they come again. And, just as eggs hatch and young robins fly away, a new set of wonders is always directly ahead. Those who spend too much time looking in the rearview mirror often end up in the ditch...

Habitats are for all of us, and the best way to enjoy yours is to plant some edibles. While the hummingbirds are buzzing the morning glories that span the arbor, I am harvesting home-grown salad greens from the containers on my terrace.

Talk about fresh! 'Red Sails' lettuce, mustard greens, and kale are but three of the many varieties I enjoy for summer salads. Rainbow chard is one of my favorite greens for autumn. Liberate the lettuce! All of these leafy greens may be added to your flower beds. "What is that?" is a frequent question about this out-of-context placement. No, you don't have to have a vegetable garden in order to have vegetables. It's your garden, and you may do as you please. I even have tomatoes between the boxwood topiaries with verbena as a purple skirt. I only have one rule: if toxic chemicals are needed to maintain a certain plant, I don't need that plant.

After gathering the greens and tomatoes, I prepare a lovely salad for myself and relax at the umbrella table. Mornings are spent here with the newspaper and a cup of coffee. It's surprising how early the hummingbirds arise! I planted red salvias along the edges of the terrace to entice them. Just through the morning glory arbor *(following pages)*, a whole new garden awaits. I do believe I see a brace of frilly kale in the distance...

Random fieldstone forms the front path which is lined with white alyssum, 'Sparkler' carex, purple verbena, 'Millennium' allium, golden spirea, and red barberry. Between its cracks are all sorts of low sedum and golden creeping jenny. This living pathway is tough enough to take foot traffic without damage, and when Jack Frost comes a courtin', the sedums shine like jewels.

You planted the morning glory, but you didn't teach it how to climb.

You grew the moonflowers, but you didn't hang the moon.

You put up the birdhouse, but you didn't hatch the eggs.

You made a bed for the flowers, and, perhaps, you made the child who picked them.

FIREWORKS

Who doesn't love a floral tribute? There are flowers and then there are *flowers*. All are not created equal, but even some of the most common are still favorites and for good reason.

New varieties of old favorites can solve some of the problems associated with their ancestors. The traditional red-hot poker (*kniphofia*) is now available in varieties that bloom the entire summer and come in festive frozen drink colors like 'Papaya' (*right*). Its beautiful blooms go from early summer to frost, and its interesting structure helps anchor the border by providing stunning focal points.

All of the contents of the garden needn't be rare and unusual, but a few class clowns can certainly break the monotony. Exotic passion flowers and common climbing sweet peas are both at the top of the list of flowers most noticed within a garden. Today's lesson: you can come from the wrong side of the tracks and still become a star.

All of the flowers presented within this chapter are guaranteed to please even the plant snobs among us. New ideas and old fashioned notions receive equal treatment. It's like having a diversified stock portfolio. Spread the risk, and reap the margin. Take *that* to the bank!

And speaking of floral tributes, the flowers from your own garden are as different as your heirloom tomatoes are from those at the grocery store. You bought how many bunches of alstroemeria this year? Are those baked or store-bought? You get the picture.

If you enjoy being kind to yourself, add plants to your garden that produce an array of blossoms and foliage suitable for cutting. Bits of morning glory vine work beautifully and add that look of an Old Master painting to your arrangement. Casual looseness improves the look of the composition by injecting whimsy, and even weeds from the ditch sometimes make it into my vases. Don't be afraid to be daring: cogs in cubicles rarely enjoy the spotlight.

Roses are just dandy, especially if you choose varieties that are resistant to blackspot like the 'Peach Drift' roses in this arrangement. Hydrangea blooms are great filler and help to anchor the more delicate blossoms like agastache and verbena. Also, when the arrangement has finally expired, pull out the hydrangeas to dry and enjoy them for another year or two.

Passion flowers and sweet peas are among the most loved of all climbers. The fragrant sweet pea is often found in bridal bouquets as well as along roadsides. Childhood memories would not be complete without them – or the recollection of making a ballerina out of a passion flower.

"Dahlias, darling, dahlias!" she informed me. I was spending the summer between the eleventh and twelfth grades in Dundee, Scotland, and my host was showing me her flower garden. I thought I had never seen anything like these before, and then I remembered that my grandmother grew them in tomato cages. They were pretty but seemed so utilitarian. She cut them for the table as she gathered the tomatoes and peppers that were in adjacent rows. A front-and-center presentation of dahlias was so out of context that I failed to recognize them.

This juxtaposition creates an odd memory for me. On one hand, I see my grandmother in her vegetable/cutting garden and on the other I remember Scotland where I tasted gooseberries for the first time. Sometimes I feel a cool breeze and it takes me right back to Dundee, but a thunderstorm will always remind me of Mississippi. Such are memories.

Each September when I am in Colorado, The Aspen City Market has a big flower stand with buckets full of enormous dahlias alongside zinnias, cosmos, celosia, sunflowers, and sweet peas. This is their best time, even in Colorado. The smell of apples fills the air of the market, and the bins are brimming with sugar beets and other seasonal root crops. I have been known to put floral sticks in these fruits and vegetables and use them in harvest arrangements.

When the dream came
I held my breath with my eyes closed.
I went insane
Like a smoke ring day when the wind blows.
                                    Buffalo Springfield

Treat the dahlia like the diva it is. Generally, the large flowering varieties need to be staked which is why my grandmother simply put them in tomato cages. To support those Scottish dahlias, my friend used green bamboo sticks and green twine which were almost invisible. The trick is to hide the mechanics of any supports you might be using unless that support is a decorative part of the arrangement. Be stylish about it. I mean, would you use an old stocking to hold up your pants instead of buying a belt?

Is there a better cut flower than the zinnia? If I offered a bouquet of florist roses in a vase, I would still prefer a mason jar full of colorful zinnias. They are easily grown from seed, come in all sorts of colors, and last for days after cutting. Other seed-grown and deer-resistant annuals include cleome (spider flower), four o'clocks, and cosmos. Like daylilies, cosmos beds can be seen along the highways because they are durable, carefree, and simply gorgeous – just as they were in the opening scene of *The Color Purple*.

Zinnias have been around for decades and still aren't out of style. If you are on a budget, a small packet of seeds will go a long way. I remember seeing them on the rotating racks at the feed store. The pictures on the seed envelopes made me want to buy all of them. The old tall varieties are the best for cutting, but there are now dwarf forms for container gardening as well as the front of the border.

Nothing dresses up a picnic table like a jar of zinnias. Cleome and cosmos blooms are natural companions, and sprigs of mint can be added to the arrangement to provide fragrance for this bunch of perfume-free beauties. I like to have a bed full of these annuals to share with friends and neighbors. Next time you go to a party, take a vase of your own flowers and, perhaps, a small basket of heirloom tomatoes. This may seem old fashioned, but thoughtful offerings are always in style.

If you are inclined towards daisy-like flowers, the best perennial of the bunch is the recent introduction, Echinacea 'Cheyenne Spirit'. This cone flower (*right*) comes in a vast array of bright colors that rival even the zinnias. The deer aren't interested in them, either. Grow these in full sun to slight shade, and they will provide years of beauty. They have the longest life of any perennial cut flower I have ever used. The woody stems of the coneflowers do not require staking, and in fall their seed heads attract scores of gold finches which join the lingering butterflies and hummingbirds as part of the magic in the garden.

206

As the color of the sky and the sea, blue simply surrounds us. For gardeners, having "the blues" is a good thing. Few flowers actually hit the mark, but grape hyacinths (above) and German iris ('Breakers', right) are among the best. Look for true blue in salvias, morning glories, hydrangeas, petunias, verbena, and asters.

Bold flowers such as the sunflower are iconic, and nothing fills a picture frame quite like the golden sunburst of this annual. Many varieties exist in all sizes and colors.

When I was a child I was given some gourd seeds by one of my teachers. They sprouted in two days and my brother and I had a contest to see who could grow the tallest plant. For a memorable project such as ours, plant some sunflower seeds with a youngster and chart the progress as the plants stretch to full height – often over eight feet. As the blooms mature and the petals fall off, the remaining black centers will ripen into big discs of sunflower seeds.

> Inside every man lives the seed of
>   a flower.
> If he looks within, he finds beauty
>   and power.
> Les Fleurs, *as sung by Minnie Riperton*

The seeds are excellent for snacks after roasting, but the birds like them in their natural state. Once you have added some to your bird feeder, your garden will become a study in red, full of cardinals who have arrived for their favorite dish.

Don't forget the pansies! Children love their happy faces, and I have pictures of myself picking some when I was about three years old. They have a unique smell that reminds me of my mother who planted them for me.

212

Appreciation

Linda Bernard - my friend and wonderful editor

Kelly Donahue - My garden responds to your tender touch AND strong back.

Doug Welty - leader of "The Sultans of Horticulture"

Sammy McClellan - We'll walk the pipe, again.

Kofi Ampofo - the hardest working man in the garden

Roxanne DePalma - for her hugs, support, and "can-do" mentality

Aaron Bennett - our stylish "little man"

Amy and Brian Pennington - I can never repay your generosity.

Laurette and Kit Kittle - Simply fabulous!

Brenda Lee - "Little Miss Dynamite", I have a rose with your name on it.

Jim and Donna Barksdale - Thanks for providing a canvas for Allen Burrows, our artist-in-residence.

Chris and Alice Holbrook - I love your little corner of Heaven.

Bill and Gayle Jefferis - my kind, decent, and tolerant neighbors

Ray Harris - my wizard of all things technical

Dr. Jason Myerson - provider of the brightest smiles

Alease Fisher - best friends for life

John and Sharon Holland - I count on you every day, and you fill my life with joy.

The Franks: Ramsey, Suzanne, and Ramsey, Jr. - Thanks for taking me in…the boat, the plane, and the Aston Martin!

John and Patricia Chadwick - Come see me, again.

Gary and Linda Cobb - Thanks for The Chelsea Flower Show and so much more.

Tommy and Dee Hilfiger - I still have ideas...

Cindy Rinfret - a loyal and beautiful friend

Deborah Royce - You were the first to read *Pleasure Gardens* and report back. Here is *my* report…Hydrangea 'Ocean House' is officially in development.

Barbara King - for her stylish wisdom and for her son, Kyle, who provides a happy home for my Dutch-dog

And especially, Theodore Rousseau, whose paintings taught me to appreciate the beauty in starkness and the magic that occurs when ephemerals visit.

Hazel

This little lady is my youngest friend, and we garden together. • *Hazel loves being outdoors and especially loves flowers. When I asked if she would like to have her picture taken, she rushed to the hydrangeas and struck a pose!* • *One day while helping me plant a Japanese maple, we found a big worm. After a bit of anxiety, she held it in the palm of her hand and grinned. We put the worm next to the new maple, and it wriggled underneath the mulch, much to Hazel's delight.* • *Afterwards, I said, "Let's go inside and have some ice cream." Hazel reminded me we still needed to water our tree, to which I replied, "It's supposed to rain tonight." She just looked at me and said, "What if it doesn't?"*

The wisdom of a child!